50 Positive Habits

Great Habits to transform your life

By Michael Chapman

http://PersonalityDevelopmentMastery.com

Personality Development Mastery - 2016

DISCLAIMER

This book details the author's personal experiences with and opinions about right-brained learning. The author is not licensed as an educational consultant, teacher, psychologist, or psychiatrist.

The author and publisher are providing this book and its contents on an "as is" basis and make no representations or warranties of any kind with respect to this book or its contents. The author and publisher disclaim all such representations and warranties, including for example warranties of merchantability and educational or medical advice for a particular purpose. In addition, the author and publisher do not represent or warrant that the information accessible via this book is accurate, complete or current.

The statements made about products and services have not been evaluated by the U.S. government. Please consult with your own legal or accounting professional regarding the suggestions and recommendations made in this book.

Except as specifically stated in this book, neither the author or publisher, nor any authors, contributors, or other representatives will be liable for damages arising out of or in connection with the use of this book. This is a comprehensive limitation of liability that applies to all damages of any kind, including (without limitation) compensatory; direct, indirect or consequential damages; loss of data, income or profit; loss of or damage to property and claims of third parties.

You understand that this book is not intended as a substitute for consultation with a licensed medical, educational, legal or accounting professional. Before you begin any change in your lifestyle in any way, you will consult a licensed professional to ensure that you are doing what's best for your situation.

This book provides content related to educational, medical, and psychological topics. As such, use of this book implies your acceptance of this disclaimer.

Table of Contents

Introduction

First off, thank you for taking the time to download this guide. This means that you are actively interested in learning about the power and methodology of positive actions in your life. Without a doubt, this is one of the most powerful and effective ways that you can empower, strengthen and grow your business, lifestyle and personality for years to come.

Like everything else in life, though, being positive needs the right mentality. In this book we are going to further investigate this mentality and make sure that we can impress it on those around us. Everything we want to do, and everything we wish to achieve, needs to be driven by the power of positivity.

Here, we're going to break down why that positivity matters ad why you can use it. More importantly, we are going to break down the five most important sectors of your life that a positive attitude can improve. We'll help you see how you can change your fitness, your mentality, your emotions, your lifestyle and your productivity. Through these tips and ideas, you can infuse your entire lifestyle with a more positive way of looking at the world.

In this book, you will receive plenty of help and benefits, making it easier than ever to change your mindset and mentality. You'll get help with the following;

- Ideas on how to stay fit and how to start moving yourself towards a fitter, fairer state of body and mind.
- Mental habits to ensure that you have the best mindset possible moving forward to changing and improve your life.
- Emotional assistance, making sure that you can understand how to keep a clear head when you need to most.
- Lifestyle plans and habits which are all about helping you become a more steady, stable influence on your life and the world around you.

Personal habits that are bound to help you change the way that you live, think and operate.

By using this book, then, you will be sure to:

- See consistent and continued improvement in the way that you live your life and work.
- Improve your body, your mind and your mentality to help you get through tough days and make sure you can always be at you best.
- Look fitter, healthier and happier all around. Give your body and your mind the help it needs to run at peak fitness and form.

Does this sound like the kind of help that you have been looking out for? Then keep reading on. This book breaks down the importance of having more positive habits in your life.

By simply having that extra positivity in your life, you can really start to move mountains and make your life in general so much easier thanks to the major improvements it provides.

So, how do I know about this kind of stuff?

Because, much like you, I was there. I used to see everything – and I mean EVERYTHING – in a negative nature. Before long my friends, family, colleagues and clients were sick of listening to me. Everything had a "But" and nothing was allowed to pass without a negative slant. This crucially negative thinking, though, was beginning to reflect on my lifestyle, my goals and my way of thinking.

So, I thoroughly researched every part of my life that I found could be hampered by being more negative – and I found it was something that hampered everything about me. My personality, my mindset, my beliefs, my understanding of the world around me…everything was just so negative!

This is why I made the change to where I am today – and it's why you can get the same incredible change of mentality, beliefs and lifestyle. We're going to break down the easiest ways to make these changes, how to keep them in your life, and how to make sure that you can benefit from them as much as possible.

Are you ready to start learning, then? Let's take a look at how you can change your life, your mindset and your chances of success. Everything we'll be discussing can be made far more effective just by looking at how it applies to your own circumstances – I found that everything that will be mentioned fits and tallies perfectly with where I was mentally.

So, how can it help you? Let's find out!

Fitness Goals and Habits

Before we go any further, it's important to start at the main point – your body. We want to look at how you can make a positive impact in your life in terms of productivity and achieving your goals. However, I found that my mind was not ready for change – the reason being that my body was not strong enough to facilitate it.

So, I looked into fitness goals and habits that I wanted to try and emulate. I got involved with this program and quite quickly found that the tips below helped me reshape, strengthen and optimize my body for improvement.

Walking Every Day

Why Will This Help Me Become More Positive?

The first idea that I recommend you look into is going for a walk every day. Walking every day is a very useful way to give the body extra exercise.

Applying The Action For Increased Positivity

Simply go for a walk in the first half hour you are up and ready to go. A simple walk around can help get the blood flowing and improve clarity.

How Often Should I Practice?

Every day! This is something I would never recommend getting rid of. It's such a useful way to hone the body and make sure you are in fine working condition.

Life Without This Change

You'll start more days with a lack of passion in your heart and a lack of belief in yourself. Days without activity tend to be lethargic, slow and often fraught.

Life With This Change

By simply walking in the morning, though, you make sure that you get some exercise. Exercise releases endorphins which makes us happier and sharper. Walking every day improves mood; fact!

Staying Active

Why Will This Help Me Become More Positive?

I found that as a consequence of working with a computer, I spent most of my time sitting at home. By standing up every 30mins for 5mins exercise, I improved.

Applying The Action For Increased Positivity

I simply would get up and walk around the office, usually up and down the stairs to get the blood flowing in my legs to avoid any problems with circulation.

How Often Should I Practice?

Every half an hour. Even if you do it once an hour, though, you'll notice a marginal improvement in the quality of your overall fitness which will gradually keep improving.

Life Without This Change

Most of my days would start with sore legs and a lot of pain going through them, with not a lot of mobility. This would only get worse as I age.

Life With This Change

This has literally changed my life. Far more capable of getting around now and my days are more active – even my early walks feel better than they ever had!

Working Out

Why Will This Help Me Become More Positive?

I found that for just ten minutes of exercise I could work most parts of my body and give myself a much needed workout. Simply doing strength exercises really helped.

Applying The Action For Increased Positivity

Every day I would work something else; chest, legs, arms, thighs etc. and I found that it really helped to improve my mood. I also felt fitter, and more confident!

How Often Should I Practice?

I do this every day and would recommend that you do the same. The benefits can only be positive, leaving your body feeling stronger and your mind running much faster.

Life Without This Change

I just found that my quality of fitness was degrading rapidly. Without doing this, my strength would just keep weakening and my body would keep feeling lazy and lethargic longer.

Life With This Change

Every morning I feel sharper and much more alert compared to how I did. I feel stronger and am more capable of dealing with physical problems without such incredible hardship.

Jogging on the Spot

Why Will This Help Me Become More Positive?

A great little solution that I found was simply jogging on the spot for the duration of a TV program. I watch a lot of soccer and would jog then.

Applying The Action For Increased Positivity

I simply just have to stand up and start jogging. Since I am concentrating on the TV, I find that I use less mental energy and therefore can keep going.

How Often Should I Practice?

Again, I do this every single day. I find that it has a huge benefit on my overall quality of life and already my cardio is beginning to improve steadily.

Life Without This Change

I would have just kept getting worse and worse; this exercise regime helps me engage with my overall stamina more and makes it easier to stay closer to ideal fitness.

Life With This Change

A major part of my life beforehand was spent watching TV and looking at screens. This simple change has revolutionized the way that I work, improving productivity and my cardio.

Bedroom Activity

Why Will This Help Me Become More Positive?

If you are that sort of person, then a bit more 'personal time' with a loved one is just what you need. Simply by having sex more, you'll feel stronger!

Applying The Action For Increased Positivity

Regular sex is great for being a stress relief element and can even be used to relieve your body of illness as it helps to boost the immune system long-term.

How Often Should I Practice?

Well, as much as you can! There's no specific amount needed but more than what you do just now should be a suitable replacement; it really is dependent on you.

Life Without This Change

Well, you increase your chances of having worse cardiovascular health and some studies even say it could increase your chance of prostate cancer by a pretty considerable margin.

Life With This Change

I sleep better, my body is in far less pain and I just have a better quality of life. My relationship has strengthened, too, and we feel more comfortable around each other.

Finding a Habit

Why Will This Help Me Become More Positive?

One of the most powerful ways I found to help myself, though, was to use a habit. I picked up playing puzzle games and it helped to really sharpen my mind.

Applying The Action For Increased Positivity

The reason that I chose to go with a new hobby is because it helps us to really improve our fitness, and our lifestyle. New activities are good for the soul.

How Often Should I Practice?

As often as you can – it depends on what you do. If you decide to join a sports team, for example, make sure you treat it with 100% dedication.

Life Without This Change

You'll just have a far less interesting lifestyle and tend to become more annoyed and frustrated at the limited experimentations you do have. This adds some very interesting variety.

Life With This Change

With this change, though, you will begin to feel far more comfortable as a person. It adds variety to your life and ensures you'll continue to see consistent success as you start to conquer and take on new challenges in life.

Parking Away

Why Will This Help Me Become More Positive?

Whenever I have to go to the stores or to the office, I now park a few blocks away. It adds another 2-3 minutes of walking, which is useful.

Applying The Action For Increased Positivity

I chose to do this simply because it's nice to have a bit of extra exercise. It also allows for time for self-reflection before I have to go get involved.

How Often Should I Practice?

Every time you go out. I found it was just a simple but easy little habit to get into that would gradually improve fitness but help us relax in our minds.

Life Without This Change

It's not going to be an earth-shattering difference but it's just another positive action you can take; without it you'll be making no difference.

Life With This Change

You'll feel fitter, you'll go into work/shopping/etc. much less cluttered in the mind, and you'll feel better about who you are and your body in general.

Stretching Properly

Why Will This Help Me Become More Positive?

I found that one of the most useful ways for me to get into a better frame of fitness was simple doing stretching for 5 minutes' post-shower or waking.

Applying The Action For Increased Positivity

I just simply would get out of bed and stretch out my legs, my calves, my hamstrings, my arms, my neck and my back. It only took a few seconds!

How Often Should I Practice?

Every single morning. It helps you get out of the door without all of those cramps and stretches that most of us find ourselves dealing with throughout the day. Very useful for helping your body heal and rebound from pain.

Life Without This Change

Not doing this won't be a major issue, but every little helps if you want to get yourself into shape.

Life With This Change

You'll feel less strained and sore in the morning and will be more likely to get to and from your objectives in the day without feeling terrible after you're finished.

Teaming Up

Why Will This Help Me Become More Positive?

Struggling to get yourself into a good shape? Then you should definitely consider turning to running with a friend. A running buddy can make a real difference to your fitness.

Applying The Action For Increased Positivity

I found just going for that run we spoke of in the morning, but with a friend, after a few weeks of practice was good for morale and overall enjoyment.

How Often Should I Practice?

Any time that you both can; circumstances can get in the way but it should never be something that holds you back too much. Just make sure you make time when you both can.

Life Without This Change

You'll perhaps find it harder to stay in tune with your fitness goals and, like others, might be prone to giving up when the going gets tough or you start plateauing.

Life With This Change

You'll likely have a healthier body and a more steely mindset. It's easier to get through the day and exercise when working with a buddy.

Making Exercise Fun

Why Will This Help Me Become More Positive?

My main fitness challenge was making exercise fun – the best way I found was to join a sports team. Simply by playing soccer, I actually began to look forward to fitness.

Applying The Action For Increased Positivity

I train three nights a week and play on a Sunday. Regardless of what kind of sport or practice you wish to get involved with, something will appeal to you.

How Often Should I Practice?

Most people feel comfortable practicing three/four nights a week. This makes the general regime of training and fitness more positive as you have a genuine reason for doing it.

Life Without This Change

If you are someone who cannot train or get fit without a reason, then life without this will be quite tough. Having a reason like sports makes training more "meaningful".

Life With This Change

You'll feel fitter, you'll be much happier and you'll be ready to take on the world. This will make an absolutely massive difference to your overall quality of life long-term.

Mental Habits

I always found that, in my battle to conquer negativity and become more positive, that my mind was a major obstacle. So, I decided to tackle the mind and make major and progressive chance. I looked into the way that I thought about subjects and how it may have been holding me back.

The answers that I got were pretty impressive, to be honest. I found that my life was going to become far more consistent simply by making the following changes. Each suggestion will ensure you develop positive, proactive mental habits that will instill you with a winning mentality.

Looking at Negativity

Why Will This Help Me Become More Positive?

One of the most powerful changes that you can make, though, is to change how you view the world around you as a whole – how do you look at negativity?

Applying The Action For Increased Positivity

I started to simply take some time to be aware how negative I was during the day. I noticed how often I would go down the negative route – everyday!

How Often Should I Practice?

Everyday. I found that the easiest way to simply change my mindset was to make myself aware of it. If I knew how negative that I was being, I might change.

Life Without This Change

You'll just continue to let those negative thoughts run in the back of your mind. If you want to avoid this then you simply need to consider making time for consideration.

Life With This Change

The main reason that I would recommend going with this change is that it helps you become aware of your mentality – how badly does it need to change here?

Thinking About Success

Why Will This Help Me Become More Positive?

Thinking about success is a great idea – simply being able to visualize what might be coming in the future is a powerful tool, and one that can improve your mentality.

Applying The Action For Increased Positivity

The easiest way to do this is to simply spend some time – 5 minutes even – thinking about your recent progress. Even if you're not "successful" yet, keep thinking this way.

How Often Should I Practice?

Every time you feel down about where you are and your progress. By making a simple adjustment you'll find it's much easier to stay on track with who you are.

Life Without This Change

You'll just continue to let the good things pass you by and pay too little attention to the good things in your life. Take the time to understand your success.

Life With This Change

Taking the time to make this change, though, will make you far more appreciative of your progress. Remember, all good things will take time to change – including your mentality itself!

Contemplation Relation

Why Will This Help Me Become More Positive?

One of the smartest changes that I ever made to my life, though, was how often I would take the time to contemplate. I used to act on impulse, negatively.

Applying The Action For Increased Positivity

By changing to contemplation before taking action, I – and you – can become more positive. It allows you to see the good, whereas taking action usually means reacting to the negatives.

How Often Should I Practice?

Every day! I found that simply taking a brief period of the day to look at where I was in my mind was a very healthy past-time, helping me focus.

Life Without This Change

I quickly noticed that failing to do this usually meant that my life would become more confusing, and I would spend too much time just reacting to situations without facts.

Life With This Change

This simple change was something that helped me to stop making mistakes. Now, I'm more calculated and take less risks, instead deciding to act on facts instead of half truths.

Noting your Positivity

Why Will This Help Me Become More Positive?

How often do you actually note in your mind that you were being positive? It's one of the most affirming actions you can possibly do when signifying your positivity.

Applying The Action For Increased Positivity

I simply found that taking five minutes of the day to look at a happy memory in the morning was a good way to change my mindset from negative to positive.

How Often Should I Practice?

Every single morning. Just a quick reminisce about something that happened in your life can be enough to get you out of bed with a smile on your face, rather than a frown.

Life Without This Change

You might find that you don't need this in your life at all – and that's totally fine. However, others will feel far more comfortable making this change.

Life With This Change

Simply taking those five minutes to noting good experiences in the past can be enough to make you feel far more comfortable with who you are, and where you're going.

Detailing the Positives

Why Will This Help Me Become More Positive?

One problem that I and others tend to have is always listing our negatives in a situation. Rather than looking at the problem, though, why not start looking for solutions?

Applying The Action For Increased Positivity

Simply swap the way of thinking around on any problem. Instead of lamenting the existence of the problem, start examining viable solutions that might help you correct this issue later!

How Often Should I Practice?

I had to do this more or less every day for a while. Eventually, though, it became second nature and instead of lamenting issues I started to appreciate finding solutions.

Life Without This Change

You'll keep feeling like the world is against you, and that there is no significant way to step forward and make your life easier. Without this change, negativity will prevail.

Life With This Change

Swapping to this change of mindset, though, will mean problems are just that; a problem. You'll keep your feet on the ground more often and will likely find solutions easier.

Challenging Assumptions

Why Will This Help Me Become More Positive?

How often do you challenge how you think about a certain situation? If you don't, then it's time to do so. Challenging assumptions will help you ensure you're always adapting.

Applying The Action For Increased Positivity

It's very easy to never challenge our beliefs and assumptions – but you could be being needlessly negative. Instead, ask yourself why that train of thought exists – and if it's legitimate.

How Often Should I Practice?

Any time you find yourself going down a negative spiral of thought. Hop online and have a look for what you're so worried about. Is the original belief you had really so applicable?

Life Without This Change

Many choose to avoid going down this route as they don't like to be told they are wrong. Being wrong, though, is not a negative – it's another learning experience!

Life With This Change

You'll feel far less entrenched and likely to be less threatened by a difference of opinion. This is one of the most positive actions that you can take.

Accepting Your Success

Why Will This Help Me Become More Positive?

Many of us – me included for a long time – simply cannot accept when we are a success. We like to think luck was involved, or that it was a mistake.

Applying The Action For Increased Positivity

If this is how you feel then the next time it comes around in your head, ask a few people that you trust to give you the truthful answer back.

How Often Should I Practice?

Whenever you feel this crisis of confidence coming on. It's a dangerous problem and one that will just make you feel worse most likely. Avoid it by asking whenever it comes on.

Life Without This Change

You'll continue to knock down your achievements whilst fixating on your failures. This builds a negative mindset and is the worst direction to go down for a positive action-driven life.

Life With This Change

You'll become far more comfortable, and aware, of your successes and failures in life. This will ensure you can continue to develop, without always seeing yourself as failing.

Reviewing your Failures

Why Will This Help Me Become More Positive?

By taking the time to actually look at *why* you failed, you can find it much easier to find solutions. Many of us know that we failed – but why?

Applying The Action For Increased Positivity

Simply sit down and write down five reasons why you failed. Now, you know what you have to work on; it might hurt doing this but it's about as positive an action as you can get.

How Often Should I Practice?

Taking this on is going to make your life much easier than ever before – so do it every time you fail. Failure is a journey, not the destination!

Life Without This Change

If you don't try to change this then you can prepare for a life of self-deprecating and a lack of self-belief. By reviewing failure, solutions become viable.

Life With This Change

By looking and reviewing your success and failure it will become much easier to stay on the right track. It'll also greatly increase the chances of finding a long-term solution.

Mind Games

Why Will This Help Me Become More Positive?

How often do you just memorize a little poem or a piece of writing? Doing this can be a very powerful way to make sure you've always got a challenge.

Applying The Action For Increased Positivity

Challenges are great for helping us learn salient points and words of wisdom. Take a poem from the internet every morning and try to memorize the words by the days end.

How Often Should I Practice?

Every day – even if you feel more comfortable working with one poem per week, do it. Challenges are excellent and help us see our own skills and talents accordingly.

Life Without This Change

You'll doubt your ability to learn and take on new skills. By memorizing a new poem every week, you also improve your overall knowledge of culture and arts accordingly.

Life With This Change

Going down this route is very useful as it will ensure that you can get the help you need to showcase your mental and memory skills, if you doubt they exist.

Force of Attraction

Why Will This Help Me Become More Positive?

Have you ever spent the day just wishing for something to be? If not, you have to begin. Spend 5-10 minutes at night just dreaming of what you want in life.

Applying The Action For Increased Positivity

The reason for doing this is simple; just drop into your mind and you'll see what you really want. Let your fantasies take control and you'll find fresh ambition.

How Often Should I Practice?

Every day! Any days which are spent not in pursuit of these goals and reaching them is a day wasted. You should always have a goal which is driven by desire.

Life Without This Change

You'll likely never have a solid and significant path to follow. Without knowing what you want to achieve it will naturally become harder to achieve those goals in time.

Life With This Change

By creating a clear part of your mind where this is addressed, though, you should find it easier to visualize and then work towards the thing you want in life.

Emotional Habits

To be a success you need to be in full control of your emotions. However, most people can struggle to get to this point – so, in this section, I've broken down some of the tips I used to get there. Positive actions and changes in your life needs to have a strong baseline behind it and it's something that matters massively for a strong, secure lifestyle.

To make you are affecting your life in as many ways as you can try and use some of the topics and tips below that I used to balance and alleviate your minds madness!

Meditate for Success

Why Will This Help Me Become More Positive?

As I continued to try and change elements of my personal life, one of the major issues that I found was that my mind was always full – meditation helps.

Applying The Action For Increased Positivity

This is the magic of meditation; there is no set one way to do it, no magic trick. You do it in the way that suits you best, nobody else.

How Often Should I Practice?

Every single day. It has been the single greatest change that I have made to my life – meditation has helped me to clear my mind of junk, and become more positive.

Life Without This Change

I genuinely don't want to go back to that – and once you have meditated, neither will you. Concentration, motivation and overall ability to succeed goes through the roof when meditating.

Life With This Change

Life with the change that this will bring is like a new beginning entirely – it changed my entire perspective on the world. Now, I'm more upbeat and take considerations seriously.

Diaphragmatic Breathing

Why Will This Help Me Become More Positive?

I began to use diaphragmatic breathing two years ago and it has helped me to calm down, take stock of situations, and deal with situations in a mature, rational manner.

Applying The Action For Increased Positivity

All you need to do is learn how to take deep breaths in a slow manner. We all have our own preference of depth and time, so check online to find help in diaphragmatic breathing in a way you feel comfortable with.

How Often Should I Practice?

Every day – once you get the knack of this breathing technique you'll want to be using it all the time. It's a great way to clear the mind and just break free of your struggles for a moment.

Life Without This Change

I found that my days were more hectic and that I would go from one problem to the next. This allows me to analytically solve problems.

Life With This Change

I feel happier, healthier, more confident when in trouble, and sharper than ever before!

Walking Meditation

Why Will This Help Me Become More Positive?

A simple technique that I was shown by a friend was to go through with the practice of daily walking meditation, which is a skill I've been using every day.

Applying The Action For Increased Positivity

The easiest way to learn about walking meditation is to check out this guide. In the guide you'll see how it can help you out in general and improve function.

How Often Should I Practice?

Basically, I practiced this every day for about two months. From there I started to really change the way that I was operating and soon became far more comfortable dealing with tricky subjects.

Life Without This Change

I believe that without this change I would still be quite erratic and likely to walk into errors that could have been avoided. With the help of this form of meditation, it's easier to get mental clarity even when busy.

Life With This Change

Now, problems are no longer such an obstacle as I approach them with a rested, balanced mind.

Identifying Emotions

Why Will This Help Me Become More Positive?

A major issue that I and many others face is a struggle to portray and understand our emotions. Does this sound like a problem you are facing? Then simple identification helps.

Applying The Action For Increased Positivity

Take four or five words to describe how you feel, and research them all online. By doing this I find it easier to identify where I'm at emotionally.

How Often Should I Practice?

I now do this on a daily basis – it just helps me to work out where I am in my mind. A re-framing of the thought can be enough to make it easier to get through a problem with minimal fuss.

Life Without This Change

Life without this kind of change is quite tough; I would find it hard to revert now. However, it mainly helps as it allows me to know exactly how I really feel.

Life With This Change

Now, I am less likely to react negatively to a situation, instead being able to analyze before deciding.

Putting Perspective Together

Why Will This Help Me Become More Positive?

One of the most important elements of those days where negativity is winning is to take 10 minutes just to put things into perspective, helping me appreciate success and failure.

Applying The Action For Increased Positivity

The reason why this matters to me so much is because it's so easy; simply take a look at your own situation, and Google it. I guarantee you'll find someone in a far worse situation, unable to get out from it.

How Often Should I Practice?

I do this on the days when I feel like I cannot muster any positivity. A bit of perspective helps us realize just how much we appear to be overblowing situations.

Life Without This Change

Life without going through this change would be pretty tough now! Such a simple way of reflecting my insecurities can be immensely powerful.

Life With This Change

Now, I'm less likely to get caught up in invalidated wallowing and am more likely to strive on, battle through, and find an active solution.

5 Minute Breaks

Why Will This Help Me Become More Positive?

How often do you find that your mind is shot but you try and work on? I've wasted many hours of my life doing this. Simply stopping for a 5 minute break can help you avoid this problem.

Applying The Action For Increased Positivity

The break is easy to apply – shut the screen, lock the PC, and close your eyes. If you work physically, just take a brief moment to close your eyes and work out what's next.

How Often Should I Practice?

I used to do this most days, and it eventually became a habit. For every hour that you work a quick five minute resting of the eyes allows you to recalibrate before continuing.

Life Without This Change

You'll likely find yourself working at half capacity when you feel tired, which is a common reason why we all feel o negative.

Life With This Change

If you make this change, you'll be far less likely to actually continue making mistakes and will be more accurate when working.

You Are What You Eat

Why Will This Help Me Become More Positive?

Many of us look to blame our bodies for putting on weight. Accepting that our food plays a critical role in life is a simple starting point for positive thinking.

Applying The Action For Increased Positivity

The idea here is simple – look at what you eat, and realize how much it plays a part in how you feel. What we eat determines how we feel during the day, after all!

How Often Should I Practice?

Take a note of what you eat for two weeks, as well as brief nots on how you felt. Record how your food appears to be affecting or limiting your emotions, and whether it may have to change.

Life Without This Change

Life without putting this change in place can be quite tough to come to come to terms with. Your lack of mobility and your overall quality of life will be reduced as you never address why you feel that way.

Life With This Change

Life becomes easier when we eat right – simple! If you give your body the right kind of nutrition and help, then it's bound to get through the day better. If we feed our bodies right, then problems and negativity will be less of a burden to fix. If there is one part you should introduce into your life, it's diet planning!

Handling Negative Emotions

Why Will This Help Me Become More Positive?

Handling negative emotions and confronting why they exist is better for the mind and the soul than just letting them fester. Remember these emotions are only temporary.

Applying The Action For Increased Positivity

Every time you feel yourself going down this kind of mental path, remind yourself it only lasts for a while. Sadness is never permanent; especially with a mindset against it.

How Often Should I Practice?

Every time you feel sad or down. The more you remind yourself that it's a fleeting emotion and not how you permanently feel then life becomes so much easier later.

Life Without This Change

You'll likely continue to feel like your emotions in the moment should define your day. By using emotions in this way you also greatly limit how far you can go.

Life With This Change

However, making the change means that when negative emotions come along they are less likely to hold you back as you know that, in time, these feelings will pass along.

Sitting Outside

Why Will This Help Me Become More Positive?

I found that simply ten minutes of time spent around nature reminded me how beautiful the world that we live in can be, when we stop concentrating on the negativity around us.

Applying The Action For Increased Positivity

The easiest one yet; just go and sit outside! Leave the phone inside and just appreciate the world around you. Listen to the animals and just enjoy tranquility.

How Often Should I Practice?

Every day that you have time and weather permits. Spending time outside in the world can be great for just letting the world pass you buy and letting your mind reset.

Life Without This Change

You'll continue to live your life in strict in|out methods. Instead, try and concentrate on less binary thinking and spend a little bit of each day outside enjoying reality.

Life With This Change

This improves mentality massively as you should find it much easier to appreciate where you are at as a person whilst also helping your mind slow down a little bit.

Mental Redirection

Why Will This Help Me Become More Positive?

Do you find yourself always going to the negative first? Then look at the thoughts prior to the negativity; what caused it?

Applying The Action For Increased Positivity

Basically, I found by just looking at what took me down a negative path I could find solutions and avoid that in future.

How Often Should I Practice?

It's hard; in my mind it happens a lot. Just re-directing the horror of a problem to why it occurred can be very useful, though.

Life Without This Change

You'll just continue to feel upset and angry, never looking at why negativity wins.

Life With This Change

If you change, you can start challenging negativity and finding solutions to what causes this thinking.

Lifestyle Habits

In this group we want to help people consider and understand why values matter so much. Many people don't put much stock in having good lifestyle habits, but as this section will show it can be an invaluable trait to consider.

Having a strong range of habits in day to day life will ensure you can get the kind of help that you need in terms of making sure your lifestyle can keep improving. I found that each of these habits helped me become more productive and positive at home and in the office, ensuring my day-to-day would continually improve.

What's Your Values?

Why Will This Help Me Become More Positive?

Another set of common issues is not knowing what we stand for. Having values helps us to define where we want to be and, crucially, if our mindset allows it.

Applying The Action For Increased Positivity

The best thing that I ever done was look to change my mindset. Make sure that your core decisions and values reflect the roles you want to achieve in life.

How Often Should I Practice?

It's a hard one – it takes many hours of inspection of who you are. Look at what makes up your core ideals, though, and see how your world reflects that.

Life Without This Change

Without having or knowing your main values most people will just go from day to day, never really progressing to who they want to be. They may progress, but never to where they intended.

Life With This Change

If you start to make decisions based on if it fits our values, you'll become stronger mentally and more committed to achieving your goals and dreams.

What's Your Passions?

Why Will This Help Me Become More Positive?

I found that by finally defining what my true passions in life were, I could be far more comfortable with who I was. My path, my aims and desires became clearer.

Applying The Action For Increased Positivity

To apply this action, I simply looked at what gave my stomach a jolt when I thought of it. This feeling drives me to find out more about myself.

How Often Should I Practice?

Every minute of every day – your passions should never be forgotten. Every morning, just take half an hour to think about how today will help you move towards finally achieving that passion.

Life Without This Change

You'll just go from day to day, week to week, year to year. You'll never improve or define yourself and you'll likely always go down a negative way of thinking.

Life With This Change

By using this though you become far more likely to achieve success, as you know exactly what your aims and goals are both today and in the future.

Creating a Vision

Why Will This Help Me Become More Positive?

The most powerful people have a dream, a vision. Make sure that you have a vision for where you wish to be – even the example of another person who's successful.

Applying The Action For Increased Positivity

Going through with this is very important, as it ensures you'll see continued and repeated success. Applying that action means simply spending the morning arranging what your dreams are in life.

How Often Should I Practice?

Every day if you can! Few things in life are as powerful as knowing what the dream and aim of your existence is. That half an hour can focus you for the week ahead.

Life Without This Change

Taking the time to understand what your passions and energies are going to be driven by is utterly vital – without it, we just go along from day to day.

Life With This Change

When you make this change, however, you will see consistent response and progress as you'll be more driven, with an active desire to reach your goals.

Inspiring Yourself

Why Will This Help Me Become More Positive?

The easiest way to inspire yourself, I found, was to look at all the success you have had so far. How can you get back to that level of success?

Applying The Action For Increased Positivity

To do this, simply look at where you have been in your life. How did you get there? How did you feel? What's stopping you from repeating that success today?

How Often Should I Practice?

All the time – never stop planning, preparing or hoping to find the solution that is going to infuse your future. Simply by knowing what inspired you previously, you can go again.

Life Without This Change

My life prior to ever really trying to inspire myself with previous success was very difficult. My self-esteem was ruined and I continually believed all success was just luck.

Life With This Change

Since the chance, though, I now repeat my old successes fairly regularly. I tend to find that my old success was driven by desire which is now missing when tried today.

Challenging Beliefs

Why Will This Help Me Become More Positive?

How often do you take a belief that you hold and go against it? I started to recently debate with myself and counter my own points, and it's been massive.

Applying The Action For Increased Positivity

Simply go through an argument yo would expect to have. What's the point you hold? What's the main counterpoint? Using this helps you see if you've really thought things through.

How Often Should I Practice?

All the time! Simply learning how to practice those beliefs is going to be very important. By knowing how others may react, you also fill in the blanks in your logic.

Life Without This Change

You'll just always hold the same opinions until challenged and humiliated. The path towards education and success means being prepared to struggle to get there, are you ready?

Life With This Change

When you allow this change to happen, though, the glass ceiling is shattered. You'll find it easier to locate factual and honest responses to the problems and opinions you have.

Letting Go

Why Will This Help Me Become More Positive?

Many of us, myself included, are wrapped in our worldly possessions. From our cars to our TVs, fear of loss makes us vicious. Losing that is the first step towards normality.

Applying The Action For Increased Positivity

I simply had to start giving away things at first – it was hard, but it got me to appreciate that life went on once that product left the house.

How Often Should I Practice?

I've so far given away something of value to me every week to a friend, family member or charity. It's helping me appreciate that there's more to life than sofas!

Life Without This Change

I found that without making this change I just continued to be paranoid and negative. The fear of losing my beloved possessions drove me to conservatism rather than fueling ambition.

Life With This Change

When I decided to give things away I felt emotionally liberated. If you try it yourself then you will see just how easy it is to be ambitious in other ways.

Selfish or Selfless?

Why Will This Help Me Become More Positive?

Following on from the above, a popular choice for helping to make sure that you make smart decisions in the near future is whether you should be selfless or selfish.

Applying The Action For Increased Positivity

Simply try and see how you feel when you make a decision for purely yourself, then a decision that hampers you but helps others. What made you feel better? This is the kind of person that *you* wish to be.

How Often Should I Practice?

Keep trying until you feel satisfied. From buying something you don't need to giving away a week's wages, there's plenty of ways to practice what kind of mental plan suits you best.

Life Without This Change

Taking the time to do this is going to likely make you feel far more comfortable with who you are. It'll also likely make sure that you know what kind of ambitions you should have. You cannot achieve a selfish ambition by being selfless along the way!

Life With This Change

On the flipside, you cannot do too much to help yourself if you want to be selfless and always act selfish. Finding the way that you feel suits you best is hard work but is going to leave you feeling more secure with who you are, making you feel more positive.

Stopping Yourself Short

Why Will This Help Me Become More Positive?

How often do you find that you sell yourself short? I used to always find that I limited my talents due to a negative outlook on the world in general.

Applying The Action For Increased Positivity

To change that, I simply had to look at when I was making choices. I soon noticed how often I made these choices to fit the whims of others alone.

How Often Should I Practice?

To practice, I started making decisions in the opposite manner. In the past when I would think of others, I would put myself first – and vice versa.

Life Without This Change

I found that my life before this was usually one that involved being unhappy at the expense of trying to make other people happy.

Life With This Change

However, I find that now I'm much more comfortable making choices that revolve around what I want to do instead of always trying to pander to other people.

Defeating Excuses

Why Will This Help Me Become More Positive?

A major problem I had in my mindset was always looking to use excuses as a way to avoid knowing I failed. To change this, I concentrated on my failures.

Applying The Action For Increased Positivity

I started to looked at why things went wrong, and what my own specific role was. It was the most positive action I could have taken as now I see where I went wrong and no longer blame other people.

How Often Should I Practice?

This has really helped me come to terms with who I am and the extra practice has ensured I continue to progress. I would recommend practicing this whenever you find yourself excusing a poor performance or stupid mistake on your part.

Life Without This Change

Before I started to really look at my own actions before anyone else, I led a very insecure life. I would feel threatened by everyone and secure with nobody.

Life With This Change

Now, I'm far more comfortable and have found I'm more positive than I have been, as I can see my faults.

Creating, not Reacting

Why Will This Help Me Become More Positive?

The most powerful way I have found to handle negativity is to create. I now use that energy for good.

Applying The Action For Increased Positivity

It's easy to apply – simply get into a hobby. When things go wrong turn to the hobby instead of reacting.

How Often Should I Practice?

This makes it very easy to give yourself time to consider a response, using creativity to drive your emotions.

Life Without This Change

I used to react wrongly to lots of situations and I would create tension between myself and other people in life.

Life With This Change

Now I take the time to immerse myself in the idea of what has gone wrong, creating more harmony.

Personal Habits

Alright, so in this section we want to take a look at personal habits that you can adapt. Most of these are built around the idea of business productivity. I found the most useful stamp that you can put on your life is a successful, active and busy business life!

Simplifying your Day

Why Will This Help Me Become More Positive?

The easiest way to make your days easier is to clear away mess first – organize everything so you can work without distraction.

Applying The Action For Increased Positivity

The easiest way to do this is to start in the morning, an hour before you need to get productive. By having no mess to bother you, you can just concentrate on enjoying yourself and making the most of the day.

How Often Should I Practice?

Do this every morning and you'll see major benefits. Whether it's the office or home, this works.

Life Without This Change

Without this change you'll likely notice that you have major problems staying organized. Days are determined then by how messy the place is.

Life With This Change

Making your life easier with this change is a no-brainer; it just means having to do an hours work before you start. The bonus, though, is a much easier quality of life that improves your concentration.

Establishing your Goals

Why Will This Help Me Become More Positive?

The best part of any project now for me – and you – will be to establish goals. Planning the main goals with the most challenging first will make your life much easier moving forward.

Applying The Action For Increased Positivity

The easiest way to apply this is either in the morning or the night before. Simply plan out what you believe is the most difficult task waiting for you, and work on that first.

How Often Should I Practice?

Getting rid of the hardest task each day will ensure that you have the rest of the day to work on the easier stuff. Leaving harder projects until later is asking for trouble!

Life Without This Change

I was never productive enough and my acumen would suffer as a result. My business was unable to manage itself and carry the right formula forward, and I found that each day would become a random struggle that was hard to deal with.

Life With This Change

Instead, you can change to this way of thinking – it's so much more productive it's nearly not even true. Now, I have all day to handle small problems having used my morning to deal with the real ones!

Beginning a Project

Why Will This Help Me Become More Positive?

One of the most creative ways I found to inspire my plans and ambitions was to create a project with a plan. 30 minutes per day of non-stop work helped!

Applying The Action For Increased Positivity

With this 30 minute window I would work like a beast on the project, then come back the next day. It allowed me to work on a side projects without getting frustrated or worrying it was taking up other time.

How Often Should I Practice?

I do this once per day, sometimes twice if it's a quiet day. By working on a side project as I go, it becomes much easier to understand and appreciate where I am at with it without sidetracking other works.

Life Without This Change

Without this I used to just make the same errors over and over. I'd continually walk into two projects at once, only capable of delivering 50% on each. Now, I give each project 100% at specified times.

Life With This Change

My life has changed for the better in every conceivable way since I managed this project. It has improved my consistency in business!

Developing Habits

Why Will This Help Me Become More Positive?

A major part of my transformation from positivity to negativity came from creating more positive habits. For example, I removed distractions from work like smartphones, clutter and computers.

Applying The Action For Increased Positivity

By doing this I found that my days became far more productive. By removing distractions – even just placing my phone on silent, face down – I would work much harder.

How Often Should I Practice?

Incorporate this into your day to day working and a life of annoying problems will vanish. Productivity and positive thinking soars with this mentality, ensuring you'll continue to change and adapt to face the problems head on.

Life Without This Change

I found that my life before this was simply chaotic. I would never get through a day without having to sit for an hour on Twitter; well, these problems are gone now.

Life With This Change

Now, I get through hours' worth of work without having to take a break. My mind stays on the job so I get less frustrated, making me feel less negative than before.

Determining Productivity

Why Will This Help Me Become More Positive?

The best thing I can offer to anyone reading this in terms of becoming more productive is looking at how you are when you work today – do you complain?

Applying The Action For Increased Positivity

If you are someone who always looks to complain about a situation, then look to find out why. What is making you feel that way? Also, what's the alternative view?

How Often Should I Practice?

This really helped me, when I looked at how other people may be seeing the picture. By simply being honest with myself when complaining, my wallowing would soon be over.

Life Without This Change

It's that simple, really, but without this change I would never have become more productive. I would always be put off at the first hurdle, never seeking to clear it.

Life With This Change

This change became far more effective and simplistic as time went on. I soon learned how to understand that complaining was a waste of time and energy that could be positive, instead!

Batching for Success

Why Will This Help Me Become More Positive?

The best solution I found to making my days easier and more positive was to batch tasks together. This made sure that I was delivering more with every hour worked.

Applying The Action For Increased Positivity

How so? Because my mentality had changed. By simply making sure that objects 1-4 were finished before a longer break rather than 1 alone, I soon found jobs getting finished!

How Often Should I Practice?

I made this a way of life from now on. It soon became a major part of my life and my overall planning, ensuring I always batched similar tasks together.

Life Without This Change

Without changing this I would live a life still led by negativity. I would find the slightest problem with my perceived schedule would ruin my day, making tasks take longer.

Life With This Change

I also found that by changing to this system I got through tasks in an easier style. Now, all similar tasks would fall under one banner and be dealt with swiftly.

Creating Priority

Why Will This Help Me Become More Positive?

By creating a range and list of priorities I found it much easier to get to where I had to be in my life, ensuring that my days never became overwhelming.

Applying The Action For Increased Positivity

An hour before bed I would make up a list of what the next day was to unfold with rough timescales for each, meaning that planning was made simpler.

How Often Should I Practice?

Another major part of my day now was to practice this at night. I would make sure that my plans would become ever more rigid, to see how I handled deadlines like this.

Life Without This Change

I would just be chaotic and take "good days" and "bad days" where my work would pile up and become nearly impossible to deal with later.

Life With This Change

Now, though? I can live a happier quality of life as I know that my days are more consistent. Whilst there are less "good days" the "bad days" are finished with!

Waking Earlier

Why Will This Help Me Become More Positive?

Simply setting my alarm for one hour earlier has been one of the most positive actions I have ever taken – that extra hour makes all the difference in the morning.

Applying The Action For Increased Positivity

I just change my alarm by one hour. That hour being up earlier allows me to be more productive and also allows me crucial time to awaken before work.

How Often Should I Practice?

I now do this every single day. It has been a keystone in helping every other positive action in this book come to life, ensuring that I can continue to change and improve my mentality to fit with what's needed.

Life Without This Change

Life without changing the time I woke up at was going to remain hectic. I would go into work still half-asleep and find productivity would be down across the day.

Life With This Change

This change, though, allowed me to easily avoid this problem and instead start working with a greater consistency and positivity.

Working in Bulk

Why Will This Help Me Become More Positive?

Instead of working in small groups and doing chunks, I found it was easier to work in longer bulks of 3-4 hours at a time, with less breaks in-between.

Applying The Action For Increased Positivity

The reason was quite simple – to apply this to my day I would be more productive, happier and more likely to keep a consistent level of performance rather than peaking and plowing.

How Often Should I Practice?

I just make this part of my day-to-day planning for the rest of my life. Now, I work in larger chunks with longer, more relaxing breaks.

Life Without This Change

Before I used to cram in work to reach a short break, and then spend all my break panicking. Now, I can just relax and allow the next part of the day to start.

Life With This Change

This change has helped me be more assertive and to work more productively. I'm now far less likely to take negative approaches to my working day, regardless of difficulty.

Learn to Say No

Why Will This Help Me Become More Positive?

A major issue I always had was failing to say no to people – it's hard at times, and I used to just go along with scenarios making myself deeply unhappy.

Applying The Action For Increased Positivity

To counteract this I simply started to say no – it sounds simple, but the first time I forced it out, the easier it was every time after that in future.

How Often Should I Practice?

Every time I was agreeing to something I couldn't or shouldn't be doing. It made me feel more comfortable and improved both social and business relations with many different people.

Life Without This Change

Life without making this change was very hard – I would usually find myself making mistakes or getting into situations that I had no knowledge or experience of being able to handle.

Life With This Change

Now, I feel more confident and in control of my future than ever before. I've stopped making the same mistake and instead am now living the life I intended to!

11193419R00034

Printed in Great Britain
by Amazon